DISCO

DISCO

by Lani van Ryzin

Library of Congress Cataloging in Publication Data

Van Ryzin, Lani.
Disco.

(A Concise guide)
Includes index.
SUMMARY: Provides directions, with easy-to-follow
diagrams, for four basic disco dances, plus variations. Also includes a section on the latest recording stars and a guide to starting a basic collection
of records.
1. Disco dancing—Juvenile literature. [1. Disco
dancing] I. Title.
GV1796.D57V36   793.3   78–24078
ISBN 0–531–02891–7

Diagrams by Vantage Art, Inc.

Photographs by the author

Contents

TO EVAN LOWELL CRAWFORD,
FOR HIS
ENDLESS HELP AND ENTHUSIASM.

DISCO

Discoing
Around the World

People have been dancing since the beginning of time. Every human culture that has existed has developed its own styles of moving the body in time to music or drumbeats. Some forms of dance popular today are actually hundreds of years old. Other modern dance styles have emerged strictly from today's culture. One of the most exciting movements in the history of dance is disco.

The word *discothèques* is a French word meaning record libraries. Discotheques, or discos as they are more popularly known, began in France in the 1960s as chic dancing clubs that featured recorded—not live—music. However with rock music hitting the scene at the same time, discos went comparatively unnoticed. Rock music featured less structured forms of dancing, and as it grew in popularity it promoted the concert form of entertainment, where throngs of young people would crowd into auditoriums or music halls to hear their favorite groups perform.

But more and more young people wanted to participate in music. They wanted to be a part of the sound and lights and rhythm, and not just spectators. Discos provided the opportunity and began to grow in popularity. Today there are more than 15,000 discos in the United States.

Though countries around the world differ a bit in what is currently popular, discos are amazingly the same wherever you go. France, as mentioned earlier, rightly claims to be the birthplace of discotheques. Today there are discos all over France, with American, British, and African inspired music in high popularity there.

West German disco bands are producing many of the top selling records on the market. Many German clubs feature disco music based on classical composers.

In England DJs with a truckload of lighting and sound equipment travel from place to place putting on dances. Finland also features traveling discos. By law, volume in Finnish discos may not exceed 85 decibels.

Japanese discos come in many sizes. They may be tiny coffee houses with no dance floor or huge dancing palaces with a maze of dance floors all under one roof.

The Netherlands, with its quieter disco clubs, Italy, with its emphasis on rock, soul, and jazz, and Spain, with discos that stay open all night playing international favorites as well as flamenco music, all give some clue to the worldwide popularity of disco.

Today's teens are especially enthusiastic about getting in on the fun of disco. They love the return of the big orchestra sound, the wide range of partner and line dances, and the revival of dressy clothes and light shows. And the marvelously tempting continuous music of disco makes everyone, young or old, want to get up and dance.

The Disco Sound

Danceableness is what makes music disco, according to most of today's musicians. The swelling force of a song that seems to wrap itself around an entire dance floor could only have happened with twentieth-century technology, for a good deal of disco music is electronically produced. The sound of disco is a blend of many musical styles and electronic techniques, with the common thread of a steady, danceable beat running through it all.

The first ingredient in disco music is instrumentation. Full sections of strings, brass, and percussion are just the start. Often the instrumental section of a song that you hear is an electronic combination of many recordings on top of each other, which together build up the fullness of the sound. Such techniques can give the effect of listening to a great many musicians when only a small studio orchestra is actually playing.

Vocals are usually added after the instrumental sections have been recorded. Here, too, technology can create impressive effects by overlaying voices, which can even allow a performer to harmonize with him or herself. Often what sounds like a whole group may be one singer in an echoing whirl of self-harmony. Parts of a recording can later be juggled and balanced to give the producer just the effect desired. Bass sections can be amplified to emphasize the rhythm, or the strings can be highlighted to create a swelling effect.

The modern keyboard instrument known as the synthesizer has permitted a whole new range of musical effects all by itself. Working on the principle of producing electronic waves at different frequencies and then altering or bending them, the synthesizer can imitate the sound of strings, brass, sirens, the future, and even thunderstorms. Synthesizers are often associated with the German sound in disco, though they are in common use at most studios.

Whistles, sirens, and the special percussion sounds that triangles and wood blocks make, have frequently been added to spark up the sound or to signal a change in the instrumental effect within a song.

Sometimes groups are classified by the type of sound they have. The Philadelphia sound is often associated with black soul played in full, rich symphonic tones. The German sound features a strong violin section with songs that are accompanied by whistles and synthesizers. The Latin beat refers to the disco versions of the Cha-Cha, the Tango, and the many South American rhythms that have surged into new popularity.

But what all these sounds have in common is a steady, consistent beat that makes dancing easy. Almost all disco music is in 4/4 time, which means there are four counts to each measure of the music. Sometimes the beat is carried by the drums, sometimes by the bass, but it's always there somewhere.

Until disco, most pop records were produced especially for radio disc jockeys (DJs), and the musical techniques used were geared to radio sound systems. Disco, however, opened up new possibilities in sound by requiring the use of bigger sound systems. Huge speakers, sometimes sixteen, thirty-two, or even sixty-four of them aimed at a dance floor, produced a distinctly different sound experience. Disco records had to be different. The full symphony orchestra sound combined with multiple tracking (one recording on top of another recording) have together helped give birth to the present sound of disco.

DISCO STARS

Springing out of rock n' roll, black soul, and Latin music, disco has gathered a wide array of stars that is growing daily. Some of these stars have the distinction of being the originators of the music that has come to be known as disco.

James Brown

Considered by some to be the first real disco star, James Brown belts out black soul with a steady beat that leaves little doubt he's providing real dancing music. Motown Studios, the first black recording operation to successfully break into the big time music market, introduced to the music scene many of the musicians who later laid the real base for the sound of disco. In addition to Brown, Stevie Wonder, Isaac Hayes, the Jackson Five, and Marvin Gaye all recorded for Motown. But James Brown has the distinction of having remained a steady influence on the music that would become disco through the fifties, sixties, and into the seventies.

Barry White

More than anyone else, Barry White, with his lush, velvety-sounding Love Unlimited Orchestra, made disco an identifiable form of music. The unlikely combination of a romantic, full-stringed orchestra and a husky bass voice blended to make the full swelling force of the Barry White sound. White has proved wildly popular as a live entertainer in the United States and Europe.

Van McCoy

"The Hustle" made music history in 1975 when, at the last minute, it was added to Van McCoy's *Disco Baby* album. Selling 6 million records, "The Hustle" won McCoy a Grammy Award for Best Pop Instrumental and status as a star of disco. Basically a songwriter and arranger, McCoy's Soul City Symphony, a full 32-piece orchestra, gives a lush sound often identified as the Philadelphia sound.

Eddie Kendricks

Heading for Detroit as a teenager who was determined to make the big time, Eddie Kendricks joined a group of male vocalists later to be known as the Temptations. For a while the Temptations linked up with a group of female vocalists, the Supremes, until both were signed to separate contracts by Motown. Feeling a need to go it alone, Eddie's second solo album, *People Hold On,* made him a solo star. This album contains the powerful "Girl You Need A Change of Mind," considered by many to be the best song ever recorded for dancing.

Gloria Gaynor

In 1975 the National Association of Discotheque Disc Jockeys crowned Gloria Gaynor "Queen of the Discos." Born and raised in New Jersey, Gaynor idolized

Sarah Vaughan, Nat King Cole, and Marvin Gaye. Her first single, "Honey Bee," was picked up by disco DJs. Its popularity led to a contract for her first album, *Never Can Say Goodbye,* and she was a star. Blending three songs together in one unbroken 19-minute side was a recording industry innovation that gives this album a special place in disco history.

Donna Summer
Donna Summer traces her singing career back to a Boston church, though she first sang professionally in the German production of the musical *Hair.* Having learned to speak German, Donna then performed in a number of other musicals in Germany before making her first English recording, "Love to Love You Baby." Originally a four-minute song, this record was extended to an 18-minute disco version and became an immediate hit.

The Trammps
True representatives of the Philadelphia sound, the Trammps adopted an old Judy Garland song, "Zing Went the Strings of My Heart," and have become one of the hottest current disco groups. Combining the lush, big sound of a full orchestra with an accomplished style in vocals has made the Trammps well known for their integrated sound.

The Ritchie Family
The Ritchie Family is an example of a group created by a studio. Individual singers and musicians were hired by the studio to blend into the range of Latin rhythms and black soul music that the producer wanted. By recording the old favorite "Brazil" in their own style, the Ritchie Family started the trend of reviving old hits in the big disco sound.

The BeeGees

A well-established pop group from the sixties, the BeeGees recently updated their sound and have become a top disco band. The group consists of three brothers—Barry, Maurice, and Robin Gibb—originally from Australia. In 1975 they signed on with Polydor Records and created a new style for themselves with the song "Jive Talkin." The BeeGees write all their own music and are known for their songs in the movie *Saturday Night Fever.* From this movie came the hits "Night Fever" and "How Deep Is Your Love."

Dancing Disco

If dancing is a completely new experience for you, here are a few tips that will help you look and feel good on the dance floor even before you know any steps. You can practice these movements alone or with friends.

1. Put on some music. Stand with your whole body relaxed. Flex your knees a bit. With shoulders relaxed, cock your head back a bit. Keep it high and keep your chin up. This will give you a smooth stance and a good body line.

2. Pick out the beat of the music. The drums, bass, or synthesizer is probably carrying it. Sway to the beat with your eyes closed. Feel the music going through you until you're really engulfed in it. Don't forget to keep your head high.

3. Now stop and listen to what is going on in the music. Count out the rhythm you hear. Almost all disco music has four counts. Usually you take two steps for

four counts. While counting out loud, move to the music.

4. Still counting, walk to the music's beat in a smooth, confident style. Your whole body should move and walk, not just your feet. Alternate walking forward with walking backward to the beat. Well-trained dancers check their chin as a posture clue. If the chin is up and the knees are flexed, the body usually has a graceful line.

5. Combine some walking with pausing and swaying, still counting the beat. Try several different rhythms: Latin, soul, tango, or a swing number. If the record you are listening to was sold as a disco record, it probably has a 4/4 beat. Listen for the beat, then sway, walk, and move to the music in your own pattern.

YOUR DANCE
DIRECTION GUIDE

The Hustle, the Bus Stop, the Tango, and the Lindy are taught in this chapter. You will be given the timing, dance position, and sequence of steps for each dance.

The steps will be presented in maplike diagrams to show you which foot to put where. The following chart will help you understand the directions and diagrams.

Timing ☆ The timing will tell you how to move to the music. It will give you the number of beats to each measure and the pattern of the rhythm.

Position ☆ Three basic positions will be used in these dances. They are:

Social Dance Position—
partners face each other.

Open Dance Position—
partners face out.

Solo—without partners.

The star tells you where your feet
should be when you begin the step.

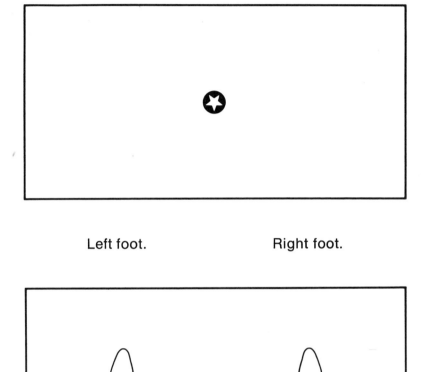

Left foot.   Right foot.

Arrows will tell you what direction
each foot should move in.

Numbers tell you the sequence of movements.

☆12☆

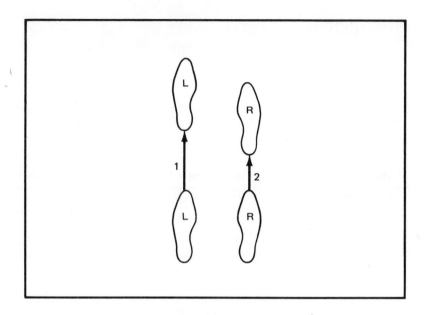

In dancing, boys have traditionally led. The leader's job is to indicate to the other person, using slight hand pressure, what direction to move in. Today either partner can lead, though who will lead should be agreed upon before beginning. This will avoid confusion.

You may find it helpful to chalk out on the floor the diagrams you see in this book. If this isn't possible, hold the book while you try the steps for the first time. Keep turning the book in the direction of the arrows as you go along so that you won't get confused and forget what step you're up to.

All the dance steps taught, as well as the initial movements described on pages 9 and 10, can be done to individual selections from the soundtrack album of the movie *Saturday Night Fever.* For the initial dance experience, "Staying Alive" is an excellent choice. Suggestions for the other dances will be given along with the dance directions.

THE HUSTLE

There are many different hustle dances—the Continental Hustle, the Latin Hustle, the American Hustle.

One of the most basic versions of this dance, the New York Hustle, is given here.

Timing ☆ 1 2 3 4 1 2 3 4

(Underlined counts are accented; that is, they receive a stronger beat.)

Position ☆ Partners face each other in social dance position. Leader has lead hand on partner's waist, not on his or her back.

Music Suggested ☆ "More Than a Woman," from *Saturday Night Fever*.

Getting Started ☆ The basic New York Hustle step is very simple. Once you learn it, try adding some of the variations. Keep your steps *tiny* and stay close to your partner.

Basic Hustle

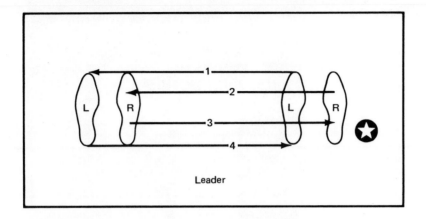

Leader

LEADER 1. Left foot steps left.
2. Right foot touches left.
3. Right foot steps right.
4. Left foot touches right.

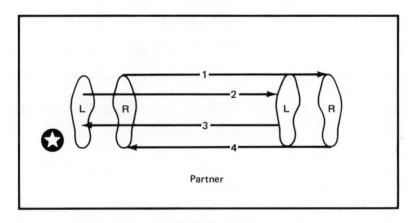

Partner

PARTNER 1. Right foot steps right.
2. Left foot touches right.
3. Left foot steps left.
4. Right foot touches left.

THE HUSTLE:
Pivoting under
raised arms.

Variations

By shifting your foot's direction a bit on the step movement, you can turn to the side easily.

☆ You and your partner can rock toward your extended hands on the first-step beat, and you can sway back on the second-step beat.

☆ Holding extended hands high and keeping the basic step, one partner can pivot under the raised arms.

☆ Now try it with both partners pivoting under the raised arms. On counts one and two, both partners pivot on the lead foot.

THE BUS STOP

The entire dance floor moves together on this fun step. The sequence of movements repeats itself four times to form a square.

Timing ☆ 1 2 3 4 1 2 3 4

Position ☆ Solo dancers form lines across the dance floor and keep in step together.

Music Suggested ☆ "Disco Inferno," from *Saturday Night Fever.*

Getting Started ☆ Practice a few steps at a time and repeat them over and over. Then add a step at a time until you have the whole sequence down pat.

Bus Stop

1. Strut forward, counting 1–2–3–4. Clap hands on the fourth count.

2. Now strut back, counting 1–2–3–4. Clap hands on the fourth count.

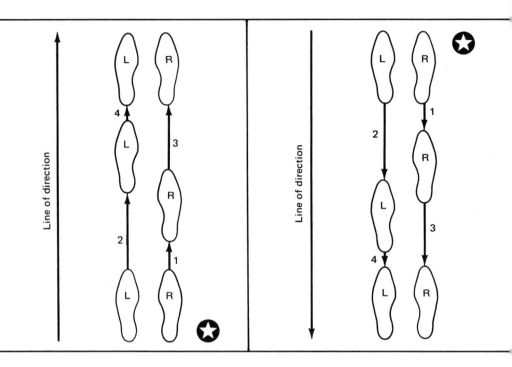

3. Repeat (1) above.

4. Repeat (2) above.

5. Right foot steps right, left foot crosses over it in front. Right foot steps right, left foot touches right.

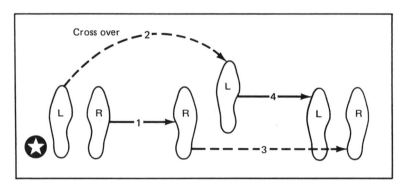

☆18☆

6. Left foot steps left, right foot crosses over it in front. Left foot steps left, right foot touches left.

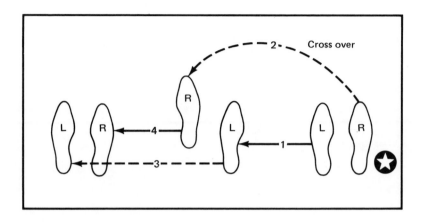

7. Right foot steps in place, left foot crosses in back with a touch. Left foot steps in place, right foot crosses in back with a touch.

8. Right foot steps in place. Left foot steps in place. Click heels twice.

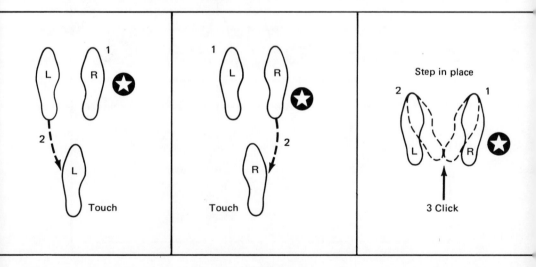

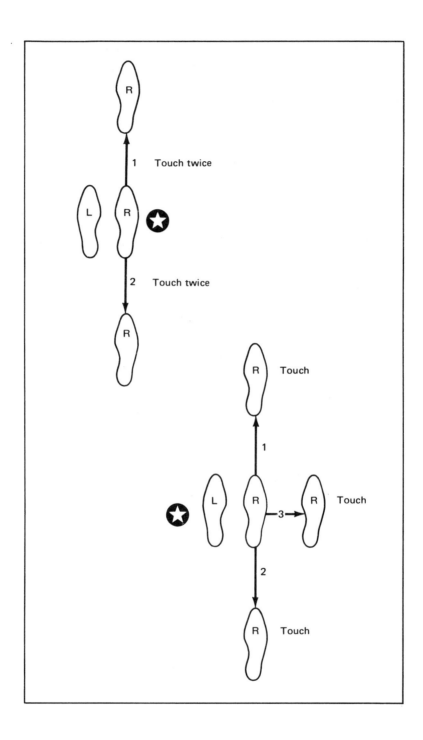

9. Touch right foot forward twice. Touch right foot back twice.

10. Touch right foot in front, then in back, then to the right. Bring right knee up and do a quarter-turn to the left.

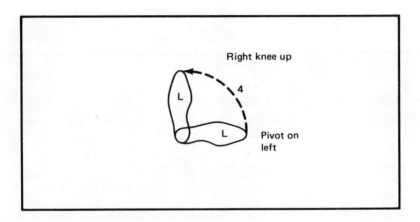

11. Do the entire sequence of steps four times. Each sequence forms one side of a square.

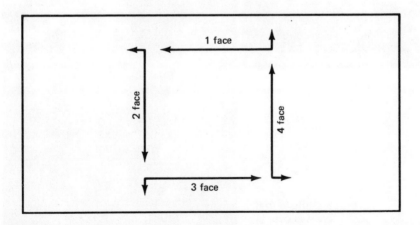

THE BUS STOP
Strutting forward.

Left foot
steps left.

Right foot
crosses over in
front of left.

Click heels together twice.

Bring right knee up and do a quarter-turn to the left.

THE TANGO

This graceful dance originated in the dancing cafés of Argentina in the early part of this century. Its dramatic moves, sleek dips, and punctuated rhythm make it a very elegant dance.

Timing ☆ |1 2| |3 4| |1| |2| |3 4|

slow   slow   quick quick   slow

Note: Two measures of music are needed to complete the pattern of the Tango rhythm.

Position ☆ Begin with the social dance position. Some steps require the open dance position, with the upper body facing at a right angle to the feet.

Music Suggested ☆ "Salsation," from *Saturday Night Fever*.

Getting Started ☆ Sleek posture is essential to the Tango. Keep your head high and your eyes looking over your partner's shoulder. Keep your movements crisp, your strides long and graceful, and your knees slightly bent.

Basic Tango

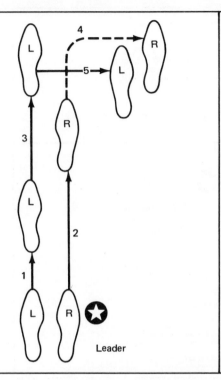

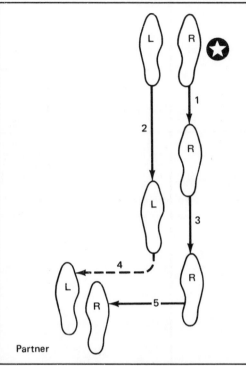

Leader

Partner

LEADER	slow	1. Left foot glides forward.
	slow	2. Right foot glides forward.
	quick	3. Left foot glides forward.
	quick	4. Right foot glides forward and to the right.
	slow	5. Left foot closes *slowly* to the arch of the right foot.

PARTNER	slow	1. Right foot glides back.
	slow	2. Left foot glides back.
	quick	3. Right foot glides back.
	quick	4. Left foot glides back and to the left.
	slow	5. Right foot closes *slowly* to the arch of the left foot.

☆25☆

The Tango Dip

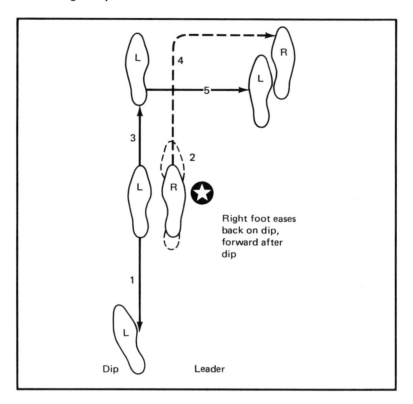

LEADER

slow 1. Left foot steps back. Right foot stays in place, right leg extended. Left knee bends as you dip back. (Right foot will slide a little, especially on deep dips, but eases back to position as you straighten up.)

slow 2. Rock forward on the right foot. Left foot stays back with toe in place. You are now back to normal position.

quick 3. Left foot glides forward.

quick 4. Right foot glides forward and to the right.

slow 5. Left foot closes *slowly* to arch of the right foot.

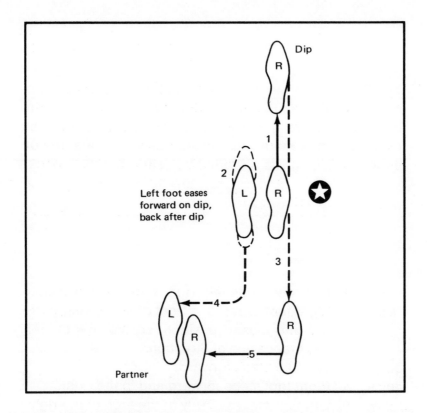

slow 1. Right foot steps forward. Left foot stays in place, left leg extended. Right knee bends as you dip forward. (Left foot will slide a little, especially on deep dips, but eases back to position as you straighten up.)

slow 2. Rock back on left foot. Right foot stays with toe in place. You are now back to normal position.

quick 3. Right foot glides back.

quick 4. Left foot glides back and to the left.

slow 5. Right foot closes *slowly* to the arch of the left foot.

The Promenade has a special position. The upper part of the body faces the line of direction, or the direction in which you are going. As you can see from the first diagram, the feet start out at right angles to the line of direction. This gives a dramatic posture to these steps.

LEADER

slow   1. Left foot steps left, right foot stays in place.

slow   2. Right foot crosses in front of left. Swing partner into closed position, so that his or her back faces line of direction.

quick   3. Left foot steps forward.

quick   4. Right foot steps forward and to the right.

slow   5. Left foot closes *slowly* to the arch of the right foot.

PARTNER

slow   1. Right foot steps right, left foot stays in place.

slow   2. Left foot crosses in front of right. Pivot to closed position, with your back facing the line of direction.

quick   3. Right foot steps back.

quick   4. Left foot steps back and to the left.

slow   5. Right foot closes *slowly* to the arch of the left foot.

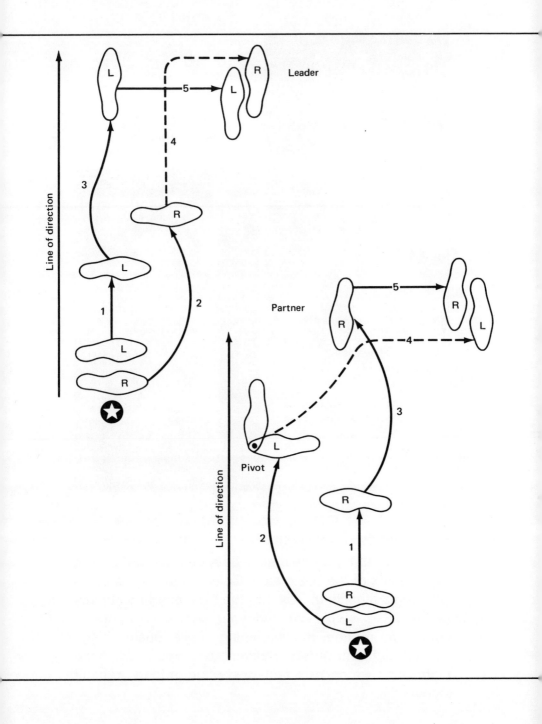

Left: the Tango Dip.

The special position for
the Tango Promenade.

Putting the Tango Together
Try simple turns by changing direction slightly on the
quick-quick of the basic step. Combine the basic steps
with some dips, then flow into the Promenade and back
to the basic step. You and your partner can create
your own routine by combining these basic Tango
parts in different orders. Remember to keep your head
high. Don't watch your feet. Just glide in long graceful
steps.

THE LINDY

The Lindy was one of the most popular dances of the fifties. As a swing dance, it has a wide variety of break-aways and pushaways, which make it an exciting dance to learn. This is a dance where experienced partners can perform really exciting to watch movements such as flips, slide-unders, and partner lifts.

Timing ☆ 1 2 3 4 1   2

slow   slow   quick quick

3 4 1 2 3   4

slow   slow   quick quick

Position ☆ Start out in open dance position.

There are frequent changes. Knees stay bent, enabling the body to maintain a bobbing, rocking movement.

Music Suggested ☆ "Boogie Shoes," from *Saturday Night Fever.*

Getting Started ☆ The basic dig step is the heart of the Lindy and may take a while to learn. Practice it over and over to the music. Be completely confident of the basic dig step before attempting any breakaways.

Basic Dig Step

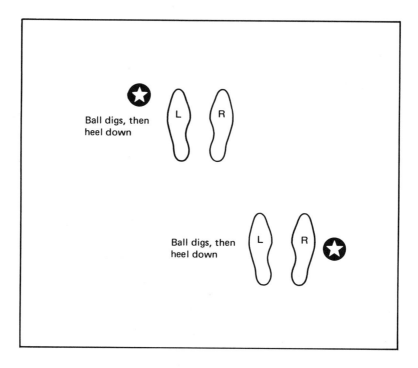

Ball digs, then heel down

Ball digs, then heel down

slow 1. Weight is on ball of right foot. Dig with the left foot as follows: Stomp with the ball of left foot (one count), then bring left heel down, shifting weight to left foot and straightening left knee.

slow 2. Weight is on the ball of left foot. Dig with ball of right foot (one count), then bring right heel down, shifting weight to right foot (one count).

quick 3. Left foot steps in place in a toe-to-heel roll.*

quick 4. Right foot steps in place in a toe-to-heel roll.

* This step is similar to the dig, but you drop your foot down much quicker and without the prominent stomp.

Lindy Breakaway

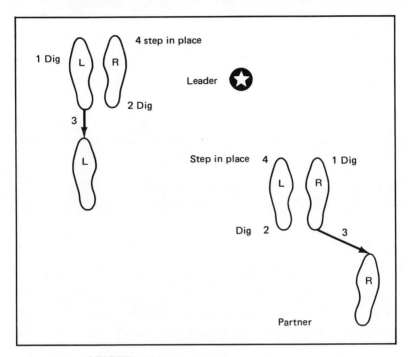

LEADER

slow   1. Left foot digs.

slow   2. Right foot digs.

quick 3. Left foot steps back as you push partner away with clasped hands.

quick 4. Right foot steps in place as you draw partner back.

PARTNER

slow   1. Right foot digs.

slow   2. Left foot digs.

quick 3. Right foot steps back as you are pushed away, hands still clasped.

quick 4. Left foot steps in place as you are pulled back.

☆33☆

Note: Leading is important in the Lindy. Your partner must have a clue as to what's happening next.

Drawing in your partner by the hands, pushing away, or guiding into turns should be indicated by quick, strong movements.

Variations

☆

Face your partner clasping both hands. Do the basic break, letting one pair of hands go and pivoting out to the side, then step back on the quick-quick. Alternate which set of hands you let go.

☆

Rock n' roll by swaying deeply to each side with your dig step, and using less sway on the quick-quick.

☆

For a turn-under, raise the clasped hands on the first dig step; partner pivots under raised arms on the second dig step. Step back, then forward on the quick-quick.

☆

Improvise. The Lindy is great for trying your own breaks and routines. Just be sure you're keeping the slow-slow–quick-quick timing.

The beginning
of the dig step.

The Lindy
breakaway.

A variation on the
Lindy breakaway—letting
go one pair of hands.

Swaying to the side
on the dig step.

Planning Your Own Disco Dance

Very few communities offer teens a place to dance on a regular basis. Often, if you want to disco, you have to organize the entire operation yourself. However, organizing things may turn out to be as much fun as the dance itself.

Schools may be more receptive to sponsoring a disco than other dances, since it involves less money than hiring a live band. Contact a school counselor or your principal for an idea of the procedures you must go through to hold a dance. It is best to do this before you begin making any plans so that you don't run into a scheduling problem or overlook any rules that will complicate things later.

Once you and your friends decide to organize a disco dance, you will want to get together to plan the event and decide who does what. Some of the things you will need to consider are equipment, decorations, supervision, DJing, publicity, and clean-up. Perhaps one person can be in charge of each aspect, with others pitching in where the help is needed.

The person in charge of supervision may act as an overall chairperson—contacting school authorities, getting permission slips and after-hour building permits signed, and finding teachers or parents willing to chaperone the dance. It is really important to establish good relations with all of the people who will be helping you sponsor your disco. One successfully run event will make it much easier to get the go-ahead for a second, or perhaps even the establishment of disco dances on a regular basis.

EQUIPMENT

The equipment person will be responsible for getting the turntables, speakers, and amps (each turntable requires an amp and two speakers), and for making sure everything is set up properly and returned to the owners in good condition. If there is a lot of equipment involved, it is a good idea to label items with masking tape so that there is no confusion when the event is over. Record racks or sturdy boxes that can hold records upright are a good way of keeping records safe and in order during the dance. Try to have a good supply of extra extension cords on hand so that last-minute changes in positioning equipment can be made easily. Check on electrical outlets and any power limitations with the person in charge of building maintenance.

DECORATING FOR DISCO

Part of the dazzle of disco is the combination of lights, mirrors, and shiny surfaces that together create the electrifying effect so many dancers love. Though the major discos have expensive sound and lighting systems, there are ways of achieving similar effects with simple equipment.

If there is to be an admission charge to your dance, some of the money should undoubtedly go for decorations.

Purchasing or borrowing supplies, checking on where things can be strung up and what the restrictions are on the use of tape and fasteners, preparing the decorations and rigging them up—all are part of the job of the decorations person.

Lights

Old Christmas tree lights are an inexpensive way of setting up a whole wraparound light system. Putting in all white or all one-color bulbs may give a more professional look, but you can use multicolored lights or whatever you have. Strings of lights can be wound around posts, doorways, the DJ booth or table, or they can be strung up to spell a word. Tacking or taping a string of lights a foot (30 cm) off the ground or at ceiling height around the entire dance floor gives a really special effect.

In stringing lights it is important to remember to place them so that no one will be tripping over extension cords. Check to see that connections are in good condition, and use electrical tape for any minor repairs.

You may want to increase the twinkle effect of the lights by adding circuit breakers. These will make the lights blink on and off at regular intervals. Hardware stores carry a variety of circuit breakers and will help you find one to fit the socket being used.

Depending on the size of the room, you may want to try black lights for visual effects. Very large rooms are difficult to light this way. Experiment. There are black floodlights as well as black light bulbs that can be used in any lamp. You might want to try putting black lights in the sockets of ceiling lights. Try decorating non-school property with some of the new paints that glow neon bright under black light.

If you know how to do electrical wiring, floodlights can be easily built using porcelain sockets and giant-sized coffee cans. Perhaps an industrial arts teacher can help you assemble your floodlights if you are not sure how. A few floodlights are all you will need for most dance areas. Aiming one at a mirror box hanging from the ceiling and another over the DJ's booth should be adequate.

Check all of your wiring carefully. Fasten all lights securely in place. Remember, when a lot of people are moving around, things can easily get knocked down and create minor disasters. Try out your whole lighting system in advance to be sure you have just the effect you want. Experimenting with lights and decorations can really tap your creativity.

Other Decorations

The key to disco decorating is glimmer and reflection. Mirrored and foiled surfaces give an alive look to the room, especially if they are well coordinated with the lighting system. Mirrors are expensive, heavy, and difficult to secure in place, but if you can get some old mirrors, treasure them. People love to watch themselves dance, so placing mirrors at various spots along the dance floor adds fun.

There are many other materials besides mirrors that reflect. Art supply stores carry heavy-duty mirror board, which is a high quality foil on stiff cardboard. It is fairly expensive, but it is also very lightweight and gives almost clear reflections. Try building boxes out of mirror board. These can be hung from the ceiling and give almost the same effect as the mirror balls used in professional clubs.

Ordinary aluminum foil can be used to cover posts, empty picture frames, or whatever you like. Taping a panel of foil behind strings of lights will give extra glimmer. Covering the entrance doors entirely with foil gives a really impressive effect.

Large refrigerator boxes can be cut and assembled to form a DJ booth. Paint the booth black or cover it with foil. Design a booth with elbowroom. Remember, it must be big enough for a table, some storage boxes, and the DJ's chair.

Tinsel Christmas streamers are perfect for hanging from the ceiling. You can also cut aluminum foil in strips and hang it from the ceiling to catch the reflections of the lights.

Keep an eye out for castoffs from store decorations. Check with store managers for window decorations they no longer want. Use your imagination. Perhaps you will be able to accumulate a treasury of decorations.

DJing

The real superstars of disco are often the DJs. Their skill in selecting records and building a sound combination that keeps the whole crowd dancing is a talent to be admired. By understanding their electronic equipment, the music, and the dancers, they can create a music experience.

Several people will probably want to be DJs. If this is true, the person in charge of supervision may consider working out shifts of DJs for the evening.

A large part of the DJ's job is the borrowing of records. Each album borrowed should be handled carefully, labeled with the owner's name, and put on a master list of what albums were borrowed from whom.

DJs working in a typical small club might have two turntables, two amplifiers, a mike, a light control board, a frequency equalizer, a mixer, a tape recorder, and a few record bins. The equipment in large disco clubs in big cities can get very elaborate, but essentially it does the same thing.

Two turntables and two amps are necessary for the continuous flow of music that has become the mark of disco. As one record is ending on one turntable, another is being phased in on the other turntable. Fading out one song and bringing up another must be done in a smooth, flowing transition. This is what marks the skill of a professional DJ.

To accomplish the smoothest transitions, a DJ readies the second record as soon as the first one starts playing. Using headphones, the DJ places the stylus (needle) on the record and rotates the record by hand until the beginning of the song is heard. The record is then stopped and backed up one half of a rotation and the stylus is replaced. One half of a rotation is about what most turntables need as start-up time. When the first song is reaching its end, the DJ must listen and carefully watch the stylus of the first record in order to decide when to begin the second record. Poor timing can result in either both songs playing at once or a gap between songs.

Making Skillful Transitions

If you will be DJing for a disco, making smooth transitions will be what you will need to learn first. This means practice ahead of time. Professional DJs have direct-drive turntables, which means that when the machine is turned on, playing speed is reached almost immediately; there is no slow warm-up time. Many home turntables do not have direct drive. You will need to check this. To do so, place the stylus on a record with the power on but the turntable still, not rotating. Now flip the switch for the turntable and watch closely to see how many revolutions it takes to reach playing speed. If your turntable takes several revolutions to reach proper playing speed, it does not have direct drive but will still work just fine. Experiment with your equipment. Try turning the volume completely down with the turntable going. Place the stylus on and then bring the volume up when you want to bring the song in. You must take care not to clip off the start of the song, as this is messy DJing.

You and a friend may want to pool your equipment for a day and set up two turntables. Practice making smooth transitions from one song to the next. Once you know your turntables and how to ready the stylus, you are on your way to being a pro.

Knowing your music is the next step. Listen carefully to records so that you can pick up cues that will tell you when each song is ending. Turning the volume down on the ending song and bringing up the next song can be done by one or two persons. Sometimes it is easier to coordinate the transition alone, but you may prefer working with a partner. Only practice will tell.

Most standard record albums have several songs in bands on each side, with a gap between songs. Since you will not want to play an entire side with such gaps, you will most likely be playing one song on that side at a time. Transitioning works the same when you're only playing one band of a record. Listen for the beginning of the music on the band you've selected. Back up the turntable to allow for start-up time and you are set to go. You must be alert for the ending, as you have less time to relax between songs. If you use albums labeled as disco albums, chances are the entire side of the record has been blended into a continuous flow of music and transitions are therefore less frequent. Remember, the goal of making skillful transitions is to keep the music continuous and not to skip a beat between songs. This means full concentration while you are manning the DJ operation.

Selecting Music
Selecting which records to play and what order to play them in takes just as much skill and is just as important to the flow as smooth transitions are. Several fast songs in a row—fast, faster, fastest—followed by a more restful slow dance is a popular pattern. Placing two or three Latin beat songs together might be effective if the crowd seems to be enjoying them. Save really popular hits and play one about every half hour to keep the excitement high.

Listening to records carefully helps cue you in to which ones sound good together. Records that use the same attention-getting effects, such as whistles or sirens, should not be played one right after another. Similarly, too many vocalists in a row can sound monotonous. You will develop skill and judgment as you practice.

In addition to being a mechanical and musical wizard, a DJ must be a crowd psychologist. Keeping an eye on what music gets everyone up dancing and what music empties the dance floor is your first step. Watch what steps or dances the crowd seems to enjoy, then play them periodically to keep everyone's interest up. Be ready to "kill" a song early if it is not a crowd-pleaser. In cases like this, your transition may not be very smooth, but that's better than playing a dead song all the way through and losing the crowd.

Light Control

In small clubs and for most teen dances, the lighting system is controlled from the DJ booth. Professionals have a full light control board with switches for light arrays, spotlights, and motor-driven mirror balls. There may also be a follower that automatically controls the lights and can synchronize them to the beat of the music.

For simpler operations you will have to figure out what control you can have over the lights. Even if you have only an on-off switch, you can get some nice effects by combining different lights or flicking a group of lights on and off in time to the music. Alternating a pattern of lights for each song may be a good idea. Special effects, such as strobes, could be saved for brief periods of time during special songs. The key to good lighting is variety. Watch how the lights are being experienced by the dancers. In stage lighting, the effects are judged by the audience. In disco the effects are judged by the dancers themselves. Lighting should add to the fun and excitement of the music.

Setting Up the DJ Booth

Since turntables are very sensitive to floor vibrations, it is critical to set up your DJ operation in a way that will prevent records from bouncing and jumping. Setting your table or booth at least 6 feet (2 m) away from the dance floor should help. You may have to rope off your area to prevent dancers from getting too close to the booth. Speakers can be set as close to the dance floor as you wish, since they are not affected by vibrations. Weighting down the table that holds your turntables may also help. Try using a few cement blocks and see if that keeps the table from vibrating during dancing.

Keeping Records in Order

After each record is played it is very important to put it back in its album cover. It's so easy in the rush of switching records to get careless and start stacking records every which way. But doing so can lead to real headaches as the dance goes on. Keeping your records in bins with the open slot of the album up will keep records from rolling out when you reach for them.

You will want to work out your own way of organizing records before a dance. Perhaps you will want to arrange all Hustles together, or Latin beats together, and so on. This is handy if someone requests a particular dance. Maybe you prefer putting records in the order you think they should be played, making sets of records that sound good together. Whatever method you choose should be agreed upon by everyone who will be working in the DJ booth so that there won't be confusion. When planning music it is good to keep in mind that it takes about five to twelve standard songs to make an hour of music. If you are using disco records with continuous songs, the playing time is usually given on the album. Extra records are always helpful to have on hand, but favorites can be repeated whenever you like.

With a little practice you will soon have all of the skills it takes to be a good DJ. Staying alert and taking your job seriously are both important. Then relax and enjoy the music.

PUBLICITY

The publicity person will decide what media to use to spread the word about your disco dance. Posters, school newspapers, and special bulletins are all good ways of publicizing the event. Part of the budget should be set aside for advertising supplies.

CLEAN-UP

Clean-up may not sound like a very glamorous job, but if all of those involved pitch in, it can be a fun time to share your excitement over the success of your dance. Establishing a good reputation with the maintenance person will ensure the possibility of future dances. Check ahead of time to see what you will be expected to clean up and what cleaning equipment you may need.

Even though tasks are divided, everyone can work on as many phases of the dance as they wish. Just make sure someone is in charge of each phase of the dance. Spending a little more time organizing things will mean a smoother, more professional dance.

If schools aren't receptive to your idea of sponsoring a disco dance, you might try working through a community or church youth group. Your school counselor may know of some organization that might be willing to work with you.

Disco Dress

Perhaps the only fashion rule for disco dress is not to follow any rule. Almost anything you think looks great will be acceptable disco dress. Though styles change almost daily, there are a few general categories of outfits that have stayed popular on the disco scene. These are glimmer and shimmer outfits, the dated look, costumes, and whatever is in.

GLAMOR OUTFITS

Glimmer and shimmer outfits typify the glamor look that has returned to peak popularity through disco. Satin or silky big-sleeved shirts and blouses, dress pants, flowing or draped skirts, and gold or silver shining fabrics are all part of the glamor look.

Since most really dressy clothes are very expensive, and you will not be getting lots of wear out of them, it pays to be clever in putting this look together. Secondhand clothing stores, church rummage sales, garage sales, and grandparents' attics are prime sources for old dress shirts and pin-striped vests and ties, as well as silky dresses and evening skirts. While you're rummaging, keep an eye out for odds and ends like drapery fringe, old dress shoes, belts, scarves, and hats. Sometimes one bargain find will create just the look you want. Always keep in mind that whatever you put together must permit free body movement while dancing.

For real glimmer you might want to purchase a spray can of gold or silver paint and spray an old pair of shoes. Even tennis shoes can be sprayed. If you're spraying leather shoes, wipe them first with a rag soaked in turpentine to remove any old oils and polishes that would prevent the paint from sticking. The paint will eventually crack or chip, but it can easily be touched up.

You can spray belts in the same way, or you might want to cover them with new fabric, using fabric glue. Adding fringe or fabric trims to outfits is a fun way to experiment with the glamor look.

DATED OUTFITS

The dated look can also begin with treasure hunts through parents' and grandparents' cast-off clothing boxes or the racks in secondhand stores. It may take a lot of searching to find what you want, but remember that sometimes even the smallest additions can change an everyday outfit to a forties or fifties look. Keep an eye out for separates that you can switch around. Looking through old photograph albums or yearbooks is a great way to gather ideas for the dated look.

Sometimes just wearing something in a different way will make it look dated. Tucking a lightweight sweater into dress pants and adding a narrow belt will give you a distinctly different look. Scarves can serve as ascots tucked into the neckline of a dress shirt.

Long silky scarves can be tied around skirts as low-slung sashes for the twenties look.

COSTUMES

Costumes are sometimes worn by professional disco performers for exhibition dancing. Couples may appear as Antony and Cleopatra or as a futuristic pair in matching silver lamé jumpsuits. Though you may not want to go to this extent in dressing for disco, there may be an occasion when costumes would be fun. They take imagination and effort, but sometimes the fun is worth it.

THE "IN" LOOK

Whatever is in is just that. Styles and trends change so quickly that the "in" look is something different almost every day. Checking magazines and TV talk shows for what guests are wearing can help alert you to new trends. Keep a sharp eye out for the little touches that make a certain look click. Suspenders may be just the thing you need to add to the clothes you already have. Try wearing suspenders with jeans and a T-shirt or with a dressy outfit. Mixing clothes in different combinations or layering unlikely go-togethers may give you an entirely new look with no purchases necessary.

GENERAL TIPS
ON DISCO DRESS

☆   Sewing skills are a boon to any wardrobe. Whether you start from scratch and sew a whole outfit or alter something you found in a secondhand store, sewing will save you money.

☆   You and your friends might want to set up a way of swapping clothes. Sew name labels in your clothes if you intend to lend them out. You might also want to consider permanent trade-offs of clothes you are tired of.

☆   Keeping clothes in order helps you see what you've got to work with. Rig up a clothesline against your wall and clip on scarves, ties, and belts. This will let you see at a glance all of the options you have when you are assembling an outfit. Grouping shirts and tops together in your closet may give you ideas on what looks good with what. With bricks and boards you can make a shelf in your closet for shoes and boots. Adding simple screw-in clothes hooks to a board will give you a rack for displaying and keeping track of hats. It just makes sense that organizing your wardrobe will make it work better for you.

Building a Disco Collection

Disco is really music history in the making, and you may want to begin a disco collection that will one day prove valuable to you, at least in memories.

Many things could be included in a disco collection: records, tapes, album covers, magazine pictures and articles, photographs of recording stars and DJs, and photos of you and your friends in memorable get-ups.

COLLECTING RECORDS

Certain records have stayed popular for so long on the disco lists that they are considered classics. A beginning collection could probably start with records that have really proved themselves. A good starter collection might include records from the following list.

STARTER COLLECTION

Where the Happy People Go ☆ The Trammps
Never Can Say Goodbye ☆ Gloria Gaynor

The Hustle and Best of Van McCoy ☆ Van McCoy
Life is Music ☆ The Ritchie Family
Four Seasons of Love ☆ Donna Summer
Disco Inferno ☆ The Trammps
Uptown Festival ☆ Shalamar
Midnight Love Affair ☆ Carol Douglas
D. C. LaRue Starring in the Tea Dance ☆ D. C. LaRue
Glorious ☆ Gloria Gaynor
Under the Influence of ☆ Love Unlimited

Check used record shops in your area. If you keep an eye out for the artists or groups that you like, you may find real bargains. Be sure to examine records carefully for scratches or dirt impacted into the grooves. Most shops are pretty honest about pricing used records according to their condition, but it always pays to examine your purchases thoroughly.

TAKING CARE OF RECORDS

Records that are taken care of properly will not only last longer, they will give you a better sound.

The number one enemy of records is heat. To prevent warping from exposure to heat, find a place to store your records that is away from heating vents and sunlight. Remove the cellophane wrapper from your albums as soon as you purchase them. Cellophane shrinks rapidly and can force an album into a warp.

Records should be stored vertically. If you do not have record racks try storing your records on a bookshelf with secure bookends. Or find sturdy boxes, old fruit crates, or milk crates that will accommodate your collection. You may want to paint the boxes to match your room or cover them with a contact surface covering.

Records should be cleaned regularly so that dust does not build up in the grooves. You may use either a cleaning brush or special cleaning cloth. While the record is rotating on the turntable, gently hold the brush or cloth at one point so that the surface dust is picked up. There are cleaning kits available that include a special fluid for cleaning records, but some record collectors prefer to use just a bit of water on the cleaning cloth.

Records can be ruined in short order by a defective needle, so it pays to check yours often. Record shops will look at your needle under a special magnifier and let you know what condition it's in. Keeping your records and needle clean and handling them properly will make them both last longer.

ORGANIZING YOUR RECORDS

Even for a small collection of albums, it's better to have things in order so that you can find what you want quickly. You might want to categorize your collection by singers or groups in alphabetical order, as they do in music shops. You could organize them by types of music. Try color-coding the edges of albums with marker pens. While you're at it, label all of your albums and records with your name. This is especially important if you swap or loan records. Invite some friends over and make a fun project out of putting your collection in order.

DISCO MEMORABILIA

Keeping a scrapbook of clippings can be fun and will help you keep in touch with new groups and trends. There are a number of entertainment magazines on the market that regularly feature articles on what's happening on the disco scene. Since buying magazines regularly can be rather expensive, you might want to check them out at your library. Of course, library copies of magazines cannot be clipped, but you can have a few pages photocopied at the library. This is a good way to collect lists of top disco hits that appear regularly in some magazines.

If you would like a photo of a recording star, you can usually obtain one from the recording company that produces that star's albums. Check your album cover for the correct address and simply write a letter to the company asking for pictures of your favorite artists. These promotional photos are usually free and may come autographed. If you cannot locate the recording studio's address, ask at your record shop for the addresses you need.

Recording companies may also produce posters of stars to promote a new album. Though these may only be available to record shops, you might try writing the recording studio for one, or have the record shop manager save one for you when he or she is ready to discard it.

DISPLAYING YOUR COLLECTION

Depending on what things you are collecting, you may want to display your collection in different ways. If you have space in your room, try creating a "Disco Wall" of clippings and photos. A scrapbook is a more compact way to store your collection and keep it in good condition. If you are a serious collector you might try jotting down the dates the articles appeared or the photos were taken, so that when you are browsing through your collection years from now you will "remember when." Whether it's for the future or for just now, building a disco collection is a great way to keep up on what's going on and to have fun at the same time.

WHERE TO GO FROM HERE

This book has given you a start on learning the steps of a few basic disco dances, organizing your own disco events, and putting together a disco wardrobe. But it's just a start.

If you are serious about becoming a good dancer, you and your friends might want to start disco classes on a regular basis through a teen club or at school. Check with those in charge of school recreation programs. Often physical education teachers will help out with dance classes. You might even consider self-taught classes, where you can just practice together and teach each other steps from diagrams in books or magazines.

If the production end of disco fascinates you, you could turn your skills toward earning money. Many teens in Europe organize their own disco groups and put on disco dances for various school and community organizations. A group is hired for an evening in much the same way a school might hire a band for a dance. Acquire some basic sound and lighting equipment and learn to smoothly coordinate a dance if you are interested in doing this. Prove your ability by coordinating several free events, and you will then be in a better position to hire out.

Wherever you go from here, enjoy yourself. That's the spirit of disco.

Index

About the Author

Lani van Ryzin, the mother of four teenagers who have their own band, is a former elementary school teacher and has conducted workshops for teachers on setting up children's learning and play environments. Lani is now a free-lance writer and works at the University of Wisconsin as a researcher in environmental studies. She is the author of one previous children's book, *Sidewalk Games,* for Raintree Limited.

Santa Clara County
LIBRARY

Renewals:

(800) 471-0991
www.santaclaracountylib.org